VERONICA RUFF

Choosing Meaningful Funeral Readings, Prayers and Hymns

A Simplified Catholic & Christian Guide for Families Making Decisions Under Pressure

Contents

INTRODUCTION

When we knew Mum's time was short, our family had very little space to think clearly. There were medical decisions, visits, conversations and quiet moments we did not want to waste. Yet alongside all of this, we were asked to choose readings, prayers and hymns for her funeral.

We knew one thing with certainty — we wanted every reading, every song and every hymn to mean something personal.

We did not want to simply choose what was handed to us. We did not want words that felt generic or hurried. We wanted Scripture and music that reflected her faith, her character and the love she had given us throughout her life.

What we discovered was how difficult it can be to find clear, simple guidance quickly. There are many beautiful passages within the Catholic and Christian tradition, but when time is limited and emotions are heightened, too much information can feel overwhelming.

This guide was created to make those decisions simpler.

The following pages follow the order of a Catholic funeral service, while remaining suitable for Christian services more broadly. Each section offers clear options, brief explanations and gentle direction, so that families can choose readings, prayers and hymns with confidence.

The aim is not to complicate the process, but to steady it.

Even in the midst of grief, it is possible to choose words that are faithful, meaningful and deeply personal.

The Order of a Catholic & Christian Funeral

When planning a Catholic or Christian funeral, it can be helpful to understand the basic structure of the service before choosing readings and music. Knowing what happens, and in what order, makes the decision-making process clearer and less overwhelming.

While details may vary slightly between parishes and Christian denominations, most services follow a similar pattern.

The Typical Order of Service

1. Entrance Hymn
2. Opening Prayer
3. First Reading (usually from the Old Testament)
4. Responsorial Psalm
5. Second Reading (from the New Testament letters)
6. Gospel Reading
7. Homily
8. Prayers of the Faithful
9. Offertory (in Catholic Mass)
10. Communion (in Catholic Mass)
11. Final Commendation
12. Recessional Hymn

In Catholic funerals that include Mass, the Liturgy of the Word (the readings) is followed by the Liturgy of the Eucharist. In Christian services without Mass, the structure may be slightly shorter but still centres around Scripture, prayer and reflection.

Who Chooses the Readings?

In most parishes, families are invited to choose:

- The First Reading
- The Responsorial Psalm
- The Second Reading
- Suggested hymns or music
- The Prayers of the Faithful (often written or adapted by the family)

The Gospel reading is usually selected by the priest or minister, although families may express a preference.

If you are unsure, your parish office or celebrant will guide you.

Why the Order Matters

Understanding the order of the service helps you make thoughtful choices.

The First Reading often sets the tone — hope, comfort, promise of eternal life.

The Psalm allows the congregation to respond in prayer.

The Second Reading usually speaks of faith, endurance, or Christian hope.

The Gospel brings the words and promise of Christ to the centre of the service.

When each reading connects meaningfully to the life of the person being remembered, the service feels personal without losing its reverence.

A Simple Approach

When time is limited, begin by asking:

- What best reflects their faith?
- What speaks to the way they lived?
- What would bring comfort to those gathered?

You do not need to choose the most complex passage. Often the simplest words are the most powerful.

In the following chapters, the readings are organised within this order of service, with guidance to help you select passages that feel appropriate for mothers, fathers, children, teenagers and adults.

The aim is not to complicate the process, but to steady it.

First Readings (Old Testament)

For a Mother

When choosing a First Reading for a mother, families often look for words that reflect love, strength, faithfulness and quiet devotion. The Old Testament offers passages that speak of enduring love, wisdom, comfort and the promise of God's care.

The First Reading sets the tone for the service. For a mother, many families prefer something gentle and reassuring rather than dramatic or heavily symbolic.

Below are passages frequently chosen for mothers, along with guidance on when they may feel most appropriate.

Proverbs 31:10–31

"A woman of noble character, who can find?"

This well-known passage honours the dignity, strength and devotion of a woman who has cared for her household with wisdom and love. It is often chosen when a mother was known for her dedication to family, steadiness and practical faith.

Because the full passage is long, many families choose selected verses rather than reading it in its entirety. It works particularly well when the intention is to celebrate her character and legacy.

Isaiah 66:13

"As a mother comforts her child, so I will comfort you."

This short but powerful verse speaks directly to the image of maternal comfort. It is especially meaningful when the focus of the service is tenderness, reassurance and God's promise of continued care.

This reading is often chosen when simplicity is preferred.

Wisdom 3:1–6

"The souls of the righteous are in the hand of God."

This passage is widely used in Catholic funerals. It speaks of peace after suffering and the promise that those who lived faithfully are held securely in God's care.

It may feel appropriate when a mother endured illness with quiet strength or when the family wishes to emphasise eternal hope.

Ecclesiastes 3:1–8

"There is a time for everything."

This reading reflects on the seasons of life — birth, growth, love and parting. It can be especially meaningful when remembering a long life well lived, acknowledging both joy and sorrow within the natural rhythm of time.

It offers perspective and calm rather than intense emotion.

A Final Thought When Choosing

When selecting a First Reading for a mother, consider:

- Was she known for her quiet strength?
- Was she gentle and comforting?
- Did she endure hardship faithfully?
- Do you want the focus to be on her character, or on God's promise?

There is no single "correct" choice. The right reading is the one that reflects her life and offers peace to those gathered.

For a Father

When choosing a First Reading for a father, families often look for passages that reflect strength, guidance, faithfulness and quiet responsibility. Many fathers are remembered not for dramatic gestures, but for steady presence and provision.

The First Reading sets the tone for the service. For a father, families often prefer passages that speak of endurance, wisdom, protection and trust in God.

Below are readings frequently chosen for fathers, with guidance on when they may feel most appropriate.

Wisdom 3:1–6

"The souls of the righteous are in the hand of God."

This passage speaks of faithful endurance and peace after suffering. It is often chosen when a father faced illness or hardship with resilience and dignity.

It emphasises eternal hope and the promise that a life lived with faith is securely held in God's care.

Ecclesiastes 3:1–8

"There is a time for everything."

This reflection on the seasons of life can be especially fitting when remembering a long life marked by work, family and commitment. It acknowledges that there is a time to build, to plant, to love and to rest.

It offers perspective and calm rather than intense emotion.

Isaiah 41:10

"Do not fear, for I am with you."

This short and reassuring verse is meaningful when a father was known for quiet strength and encouragement. It focuses on God's sustaining presence and faithfulness.

It is often chosen when simplicity is preferred.

Joshua 24:15

"As for me and my household, we will serve the Lord."

This passage is sometimes chosen when faith was central to a father's leadership within the family. It reflects commitment, guidance and a desire to live faithfully.

It may be especially appropriate when faith was actively practised in the home.

A Final Thought When Choosing

When selecting a First Reading for a father, consider:

- Was he known for quiet strength or guidance?
- Did he lead his family in faith?
- Did he endure illness or hardship with dignity?
- Do you want to focus on his character, or on God's promise?

The most meaningful reading will be the one that reflects his life and offers reassurance to those gathered.

For an Adult Woman

When choosing a First Reading for an adult woman, families often look for passages that reflect wisdom, dignity, faithfulness and inner strength. Not every woman's life is defined by motherhood; many are remembered for their character, their work, their friendships and their quiet devotion.

The First Reading should set a tone of respect and hope. For an adult woman, families often prefer passages that speak of grace, resilience and the enduring presence of God.

Below are readings that may feel appropriate in these circumstances.

Proverbs 31:10–12, 25–31

"She is clothed with strength and dignity."

Selected verses from this passage can honour a woman's character without focusing solely on domestic imagery. It reflects strength, wisdom and the respect she earned through her life.

This reading is often chosen when the intention is to acknowledge a life lived with integrity and purpose.

Wisdom 4:7–15

"The righteous, though they die early, will be at rest."

This passage may be especially meaningful when a woman's life felt shorter than expected. It speaks of dignity, peace and God's understanding of a life's fullness beyond its length.

It offers reassurance without dramatic language.

Isaiah 43:1–2

"Do not fear, for I have redeemed you; I have called you by name."

This reading emphasises personal worth and God's faithful presence. It can feel deeply comforting when remembering a woman whose identity, faith or personal journey was central to her life.

It is direct, steady and reassuring.

Song of Songs 2:10–13

"Arise, my love, my fair one, and come away."

Occasionally chosen in Christian services, this poetic passage speaks of invitation and beauty. It may be meaningful when remembering someone whose life was marked by warmth, creativity or gentleness.

Because of its lyrical tone, it is best selected when the family is comfortable with symbolic language.

A Final Thought When Choosing

When selecting a First Reading for an adult woman, consider:

- Was she known for quiet resilience?
- Did she live with visible faith and conviction?
- Was her life defined by service, creativity, leadership or friendship?
- Do you prefer something reflective, or something direct and reassuring?

The most appropriate reading will honour who she was, while offering comfort and hope to those gathered.

For an Adult Man

When choosing a First Reading for an adult man, families often look for passages that reflect integrity, faithfulness, responsibility and quiet strength. Many men are remembered for their steadiness — the way they showed up consistently for family, work and community.

The First Reading should offer respect and hope. For an adult man, families often prefer readings that speak of trust in God, perseverance and the dignity of a life lived with purpose.

Below are passages that may feel appropriate in these circumstances.

Micah 6:6–8

"What does the Lord require of you? To act justly and to love mercy and to walk humbly with your God."

This short and direct passage reflects integrity and moral steadiness. It may be especially meaningful when remembering a man known for fairness, humility or a strong sense of right and wrong.

It is simple, clear and quietly powerful.

Ecclesiastes 3:1–8

"There is a time for everything."

This reflection on the seasons of life can be fitting when remembering a life marked by work, dedication and commitment. It acknowledges the rhythm of building, planting, loving and resting.

It offers perspective and calm without emotional intensity.

Isaiah 40:28–31

"Those who hope in the Lord will renew their strength."

This passage speaks of endurance and renewal. It may be especially appropriate when a man endured illness, responsibility or hardship with perseverance.

It balances strength with reliance on God's sustaining grace.

Wisdom 3:1–6

"The souls of the righteous are in the hand of God."

Often chosen in Catholic funerals, this passage speaks of peace after struggle and the security of eternal life. It may be fitting when the focus is on faithfulness and the promise of rest.

It emphasises hope rather than loss.

A Final Thought When Choosing

When selecting a First Reading for an adult man, consider:

- Was he known for integrity and steadiness?
- Did he live his faith quietly and consistently?
- Did he endure hardship with dignity?
- Do you wish to focus on character, or on God's promise?

The right reading will honour the life he lived while offering reassurance and hope to those gathered.

For a Teenager

Choosing a First Reading for a teenager requires particular care. When a young life ends, families often struggle to find words that feel adequate. In these circumstances, simplicity and hope are usually more appropriate than complexity.

The First Reading should offer reassurance, dignity and the promise of God's presence. Many families prefer passages that speak of being known, loved and held securely by God.

Below are readings that may feel appropriate when remembering a teenager.

Isaiah 43:1–2

"Do not fear, for I have redeemed you; I have called you by name."

This passage speaks of personal identity and belonging. It may be especially meaningful when remembering a young person whose individuality, gifts or friendships were central to their life.

It is direct, steady and reassuring.

Wisdom 4:7–15

"The righteous, though they die early, will be at rest."

This reading is often chosen when a life feels far too short. It speaks gently of dignity and peace, reminding those gathered that length of years does not determine the fullness of a life in God's sight.

It offers perspective without harsh explanation.

Ecclesiastes 3:1–2

"A time to be born and a time to die."

Selected verses from this passage can provide quiet acknowledgement of life's fragility. It is best chosen when the family prefers reflection rather than detailed imagery.

It offers calm and solemnity.

Jeremiah 29:11

"For I know the plans I have for you..."

This verse is sometimes chosen in Christian services when hope and promise are central themes. It may be meaningful when remembering a young person with dreams and potential.

Because this verse is often quoted widely, families should ensure it reflects their intention and faith context.

A Final Thought When Choosing

When selecting a First Reading for a teenager, consider:

- Do you want the focus to be on identity and belonging?
- Would reassurance be more helpful than reflection?
- Does the family prefer simplicity over symbolism?

In circumstances of sudden or early loss, gentle language and clear hope are often the most comforting.

For a Child

Choosing a First Reading for a child is one of the most difficult decisions a family may face. In these circumstances, simplicity and tenderness are especially important.

The First Reading should offer reassurance, dignity and a sense of being held securely in God's care. Families often prefer passages that speak of protection, belonging and gentle promise.

Below are readings that may feel appropriate when remembering a child.

Isaiah 41:10

"Do not fear, for I am with you."

This short and steady verse speaks of God's presence and protection. It may be meaningful when the focus is on reassurance for those gathered rather than detailed reflection.

Its simplicity often makes it especially suitable.

Wisdom 3:1–3

"The souls of the righteous are in the hand of God."

Selected verses from this passage can be chosen for their gentle promise of peace. It emphasises that those who are loved by God remain secure in His care.

Families often appreciate its calm tone.

Isaiah 49:15–16

"I will not forget you... I have engraved you on the palms of my hands."

This reading speaks of being remembered and held by God. It may be especially meaningful when parents wish to emphasise that their child is known and loved beyond this life.

It carries tenderness without complexity.

Lamentations 3:22–26

"The steadfast love of the Lord never ceases."

This passage speaks of enduring mercy and quiet hope. It may be appropriate when families prefer language centred on God's compassion rather than explanation.

It is solemn but not overwhelming.

A Final Thought When Choosing

When selecting a First Reading for a child, consider:

- Would brief and simple words feel most appropriate?
- Is reassurance more helpful than reflection?
- Do you prefer language centred on protection and love?

In these circumstances, clarity and gentleness are often the most comforting.

For a Baby or Infant

Choosing a First Reading for a baby or infant requires great tenderness. In these moments, families are often overwhelmed, and the simplest words are usually the most appropriate.

The First Reading should offer reassurance and a sense of being held securely in God's love. Many families prefer passages that speak of protection, remembrance and enduring mercy.

Below are readings that may feel fitting when remembering a baby or infant.

Isaiah 49:15–16

"I will not forget you... I have engraved you on the palms of my hands."

This passage speaks of being remembered and held by God. It may be especially meaningful when parents wish to emphasise that their child is known and loved beyond earthly life.

Its language is gentle and steady.

Wisdom 3:1–3

"The souls of the righteous are in the hand of God."

Selected verses from this passage offer reassurance of peace and security. It avoids complexity and centres on God's protective care.

Families often find comfort in its quiet tone.

Psalm 23 (selected verses)

Although usually used as a Responsorial Psalm rather than a First Reading, selected verses may be referenced in Christian services. Its imagery of care and guidance can feel especially comforting.

It is familiar, simple and deeply reassuring.

Lamentations 3:22–23

"His mercies are new every morning."

This short passage speaks of enduring mercy and faithfulness. It may be chosen when families prefer language centred on compassion and hope.

It is brief and solemn.

A Final Thought When Choosing

When selecting a First Reading for a baby or infant, simplicity is often best.

- Choose shorter passages.
- Avoid complex imagery.
- Focus on reassurance and love.

There are no words that remove the pain of such loss. The most appropriate reading will be the one that gently affirms that this child is held securely in God's care.

For Sudden or Unexpected Loss

When death comes suddenly, families are often left in shock. In these circumstances, the First Reading should offer steadiness rather than explanation.

When my own father died unexpectedly, we discovered how difficult it was to find words that did not attempt to explain what could not be explained.

It is rarely helpful to choose passages that interpret events. Instead, many families prefer readings that focus on God's constant presence, protection and promise — words that remain firm when everything else feels uncertain.

Below are readings that may feel appropriate when loss was unexpected.

Isaiah 41:10

"Do not fear, for I am with you."

This brief and direct reassurance may be especially meaningful in times of sudden loss. It centres not on the event itself, but on God's presence within it.

Its simplicity offers stability when emotions are overwhelming.

Lamentations 3:22–26

"The steadfast love of the Lord never ceases."

This passage acknowledges sorrow while affirming enduring mercy. It does not avoid grief, yet it anchors hope in God's faithfulness.

It may be fitting when the family wishes to acknowledge pain without losing sight of promise.

Wisdom 4:7–15

"The righteous, though they die early, will be at rest."

Often chosen when a life feels shortened, this reading gently affirms that fullness of life is not measured in years alone.

It offers dignity and peace without dramatic language.

Psalm 121 (selected verses)

"The Lord is your keeper."

Although typically used as a Responsorial Psalm, selected verses may be referenced in Christian services. Its imagery of watchfulness and protection can feel especially steady when circumstances were unexpected.

It focuses on God's constancy rather than the details of loss.

A Final Thought When Choosing

When selecting a First Reading after sudden loss, consider:

- Do you need reassurance more than reflection?
- Would shorter, clearer passages feel steadier?
- Does the family prefer language centred on presence rather than explanation?

In times of shock, calm and direct words often provide the greatest comfort.

For Long Illness

When death follows a period of illness, families often experience a mixture of grief and relief. There may have been months or years of endurance, care and quiet courage.

In these circumstances, the First Reading can gently acknowledge that journey. Many families prefer passages that speak of perseverance, faithfulness and the promise of rest after struggle.

Below are readings that may feel appropriate when illness has been part of the story.

Wisdom 3:1–6

"The souls of the righteous are in the hand of God."
This passage is frequently chosen in Catholic funerals when a life has included suffering. It speaks of peace and security after hardship, affirming that those who endured faithfully are held safely in God's care.

It offers reassurance without dramatic language.

Isaiah 40:28–31

"Those who hope in the Lord will renew their strength."
This reading reflects perseverance and quiet reliance on God. It may be especially meaningful when a person faced illness with resilience or steady faith.

It balances acknowledgement of human weakness with divine strength.

Lamentations 3:22–23

"His mercies are new every morning."
This short passage centres on enduring compassion and faithfulness. It may be fitting when the family wishes to emphasise God's constancy throughout a difficult season.

Its tone is solemn and hopeful.

Ecclesiastes 3:1–2

"A time to be born and a time to die."

Selected verses from this passage can acknowledge the natural rhythm of life's seasons. It may feel appropriate when illness was part of a longer journey toward rest.

It offers perspective and calm.

A Final Thought When Choosing

When selecting a First Reading after long illness, consider:

- Do you wish to acknowledge perseverance and endurance?
- Would a focus on rest and peace feel appropriate?
- Do you prefer language centred on faithfulness rather than struggle?

In these circumstances, readings that speak quietly of hope and rest often bring the greatest comfort.

The Responsorial Psalm

For a Mother

When selecting a Psalm for a mother, families often prefer language that reflects care, guidance, reassurance and enduring love.

Below are psalms frequently chosen for mothers.

Psalm 23

"The Lord is my shepherd."

This is one of the most widely chosen funeral psalms. Its imagery of guidance, protection and peaceful rest makes it especially appropriate when remembering a mother who offered steadiness and care.

Its familiarity can bring comfort to those gathered.

Psalm 27

"The Lord is my light and my salvation."

This psalm speaks of trust and confidence in God's presence. It may be especially meaningful when a mother lived her faith visibly and encouraged others to do the same.

It balances strength and reassurance.

Psalm 121

"The Lord is your keeper."

This psalm reflects protection and watchfulness. It may feel appropriate when the family wishes to emphasise God's continued care beyond earthly life.

Its tone is calm and steady.

A Final Thought When Choosing

When selecting a Psalm for a mother, consider:

- Would familiar words bring comfort?
- Do you prefer imagery of guidance, light or protection?
- Does the Psalm reflect her quiet faith?

The most appropriate choice will feel both personal and prayerful.

For a Father

When selecting a Psalm for a father, families often look for language that reflects strength, trust and steadfast presence. Because the Psalm is prayed by the congregation, it can also offer reassurance to those who feel the loss most deeply.

Below are psalms frequently chosen for fathers.

Psalm 23

"The Lord is my shepherd."

This psalm speaks of guidance, provision and peaceful rest. It may feel especially appropriate when remembering a father who offered steadiness and care throughout his life.

Its familiarity often brings comfort to the family and congregation.

Psalm 27

"The Lord is my light and my salvation."
This psalm reflects confidence and trust in God, even in the face of fear. It may be meaningful when a father was known for resilience or visible faith.
It carries both strength and reassurance.

Psalm 121

"The Lord is your keeper."
This psalm speaks of watchfulness and protection. It may be chosen when the family wishes to emphasise God's continued care beyond earthly life.
Its tone is steady and prayerful.

Psalm 91

"He will command his angels concerning you."
This psalm reflects shelter and protection. It may feel appropriate when the focus is on security and trust in God's safeguarding presence.
It should be chosen thoughtfully, as its imagery is vivid.

A Final Thought When Choosing

When selecting a Psalm for a father, consider:

- Would familiar words bring reassurance?
- Do you prefer language of strength, protection or light?
- Does the Psalm reflect the tone of the service you hope to create?

Because the Psalm is prayed together, its rhythm and familiarity often provide quiet comfort.

For an Adult Woman

When selecting a Psalm for an adult woman, families often look for language that reflects dignity, grace and faithful trust. Because the Psalm becomes the shared prayer of those gathered, it can help express both remembrance and hope.

Below are psalms frequently chosen for an adult woman.

Psalm 23

"The Lord is my shepherd."

This psalm remains one of the most widely chosen at Christian funerals. Its imagery of guidance and peaceful rest can feel especially fitting when remembering a woman known for steadiness, kindness or quiet faith.

Its familiarity often brings calm to the congregation.

Psalm 46

"God is our refuge and strength."

This psalm speaks of security and confidence in God's presence. It may be meaningful when a woman demonstrated resilience, leadership or strong conviction.

It balances reassurance with strength.

Psalm 121

"The Lord is your keeper."

This psalm reflects protection and watchfulness. It may be especially appropriate when the family wishes to emphasise God's continued care and faithfulness.

Its tone is steady and prayerful.

Psalm 139

"You have searched me, Lord, and you know me."

This psalm speaks of being fully known and held by God. It may be meaningful when remembering a woman whose individuality, gifts or faith journey were central to her life.

Because of its personal tone, it can feel deeply reflective.

A Final Thought When Choosing

When selecting a Psalm for an adult woman, consider:

- Do you prefer imagery of refuge, guidance or being known by God?
- Would familiar words feel comforting to those gathered?
- Does the Psalm reflect her character and faith?

A Psalm that feels natural when prayed aloud often brings the greatest comfort.

For an Adult Man

When selecting a Psalm for an adult man, families often look for language that reflects trust, integrity and quiet strength. Because the Psalm is prayed together by the congregation, it can offer both remembrance and reassurance.

Below are psalms frequently chosen for an adult man.

Psalm 23

"The Lord is my shepherd."

This psalm speaks of guidance, provision and peaceful rest. It may feel especially appropriate when remembering a man known for steadiness and reliability.

Its familiarity often provides comfort to those gathered.

Psalm 27

"The Lord is my light and my salvation."
This psalm reflects confidence and trust in God. It may be meaningful when a man lived his faith visibly or faced life's challenges with courage.
It carries both strength and reassurance.

Psalm 121

"The Lord is your keeper."
This psalm speaks of watchfulness and protection. It may be chosen when the family wishes to emphasise God's enduring care beyond earthly life.
Its tone is steady and prayerful.

Psalm 16

"You will show me the path of life."
This psalm reflects trust and hope in God's presence. It may be especially fitting when the focus is on faithfulness and the promise of life beyond death.
It is reflective without being heavy.

A Final Thought When Choosing

When selecting a Psalm for an adult man, consider:

- Would familiar words bring comfort?
- Do you prefer language of guidance, strength or protection?
- Does the Psalm reflect the tone of faith he carried through his life?

Because the Psalm is prayed aloud, clarity and familiarity often provide the greatest reassurance.

For a Teenager

When selecting a Psalm for a teenager, families often look for language that reflects belonging, protection and hope. Because the Psalm becomes the shared prayer of those gathered, it can help express both sorrow and trust in God's presence.

In circumstances of early loss, simplicity and clarity are often most appropriate.

Below are psalms that may feel fitting when remembering a teenager.

Psalm 23

"The Lord is my shepherd."

Its familiarity and imagery of guidance and protection can bring comfort in moments of shock. It centres on care and peaceful rest rather than explanation.

It is often chosen when the family prefers steady reassurance.

Psalm 139

"You have searched me, Lord, and you know me."

This psalm speaks of being fully known and understood by God. It may be meaningful when remembering a young person whose individuality, friendships and personality were central to their life.

Its tone is personal and reflective.

Psalm 121

"The Lord is your keeper."

This psalm reflects watchfulness and protection. It may feel especially steady when the loss was unexpected.

Its language is direct and reassuring.

Psalm 34 18

"The Lord is close to the brokenhearted."

This short verse may be used within a longer psalm selection. It acknowledges sorrow while affirming God's nearness.

It is especially meaningful when the congregation needs gentle reassurance.

A Final Thought When Choosing

When selecting a Psalm for a teenager, consider:

- Would familiar language bring comfort?
- Do you prefer imagery of protection, belonging or closeness?
- Does the Psalm reflect the tone of hope you wish to express?

In circumstances of early loss, simple and steady words often speak most clearly.

For a Child

When selecting a Psalm for a child, families often look for words that are simple, reassuring and easy for the congregation to pray together. In these circumstances, clarity and gentleness are especially important.

Because Psalms are spoken or sung aloud, familiar language can bring comfort when emotions are difficult to manage.

Below are psalms that may feel appropriate when remembering a child.

Psalm 23

"The Lord is my shepherd."

This psalm is widely chosen for its imagery of care and protection. Its familiarity often provides comfort to both children and adults present at the service.

Its tone is peaceful and reassuring.

Psalm 121

"The Lord is your keeper."

This psalm speaks of watchfulness and protection. It may feel especially steady when the focus is on God's safeguarding presence.

Its language is clear and direct.

Psalm 34 18

"The Lord is close to the brokenhearted."

This short verse may be included within a fuller selection. It acknowledges sorrow while affirming God's nearness.

It is gentle without being overwhelming.

Psalm 100

"Shout for joy to the Lord, all the earth."

In certain Christian services, this psalm may be chosen when the focus is on innocence, joy and gratitude for the life that was given.

It should be selected thoughtfully, ensuring it reflects the tone the family wishes to create.

A Final Thought When Choosing

When selecting a Psalm for a child, consider:

- Would shorter and familiar words feel most appropriate?
- Is reassurance more helpful than reflection?
- Does the Psalm offer calm rather than complexity?

In these moments, simple language often carries the deepest comfort.

For a Baby or Infant

When selecting a Psalm for a baby or infant, simplicity is especially important. Families are often overwhelmed, and familiar words can provide a steady anchor within the service.

Because the Psalm is prayed together, choosing one that is widely known can help support those who may struggle to speak.

Below are psalms that may feel appropriate in these circumstances.

Psalm 23

"The Lord is my shepherd."

Its imagery of care, guidance and peaceful rest makes it one of the most commonly chosen psalms for funerals of all ages. For a baby or infant, its tone of protection and gentleness is especially fitting.

Its familiarity often brings quiet comfort.

Psalm 121

"The Lord is your keeper."

This psalm reflects watchfulness and protection. It may be chosen when the focus is on God's safeguarding presence.

Its language is clear and steady.

Psalm 131

"I have calmed and quieted my soul."

This short psalm carries a tone of peace and trust. It may feel especially appropriate when the family prefers something brief and reflective.

Its simplicity can be deeply moving.

A Final Thought When Choosing

When selecting a Psalm for a baby or infant, shorter passages and familiar language are often most appropriate.

Choose words that feel gentle when spoken aloud. In these circumstances, calm and clarity provide the greatest reassurance.

For Sudden or Unexpected Loss

When death comes suddenly, families are often in shock. In these circumstances, the Psalm should offer steadiness rather than interpretation.

Because the Psalm is prayed aloud by the congregation, familiar and direct language can provide stability when emotions are unsettled.

Below are psalms that may feel appropriate when loss was unexpected.

Psalm 23

"The Lord is my shepherd."

Its imagery of guidance and peaceful rest can feel especially grounding in moments of shock. It centres on care rather than explanation.

Its familiarity often provides comfort.

Psalm 121

"The Lord is your keeper."

This psalm reflects watchfulness and protection. It may feel especially steady when circumstances were sudden or difficult to understand.

Its language is clear and reassuring.

Psalm 46

"God is our refuge and strength."

This psalm speaks of security even when "the earth gives way." It may be meaningful when the family wishes to acknowledge instability while affirming God's presence.

Its tone is strong yet composed.

Psalm 34 18

"The Lord is close to the brokenhearted."

This short verse may be included within a fuller selection. It directly acknowledges sorrow while affirming nearness.

It is simple and steady.

A Final Thought When Choosing

When selecting a Psalm after sudden loss, consider:

- Would familiar words bring stability?
- Is reassurance more helpful than reflection?
- Does the Psalm feel steady when prayed aloud?

In times of shock, calm and recognisable language often provides the greatest comfort.

For Long Illness

When death follows a period of illness, families often carry both grief and a sense of release after a long journey. In these circumstances, the Psalm can gently acknowledge endurance while turning the focus toward peace and trust.

Because the Psalm is prayed together, choosing language that reflects steadiness and hope can help unify the service.

Below are psalms that may feel appropriate when illness has been part of the story.

Psalm 23

"The Lord is my shepherd."

Its imagery of guidance through "the valley of the shadow" and into rest makes it especially fitting after a long struggle. It speaks quietly of presence through difficulty.

Its familiarity often brings comfort.

Psalm 30

"You turned my mourning into dancing."

This psalm reflects transition from sorrow to hope. It may feel meaningful when the family wishes to acknowledge hardship while affirming God's faithfulness beyond it.

It should be chosen thoughtfully to ensure the tone suits the service.

Psalm 62

"My soul finds rest in God alone."

This psalm centres on quiet trust and rest. It may be especially appropriate when a long illness has led to weariness, and the focus is now on peace.

Its tone is calm and reflective.

Psalm 103

"The Lord is compassionate and gracious."

This psalm speaks of mercy and enduring love. It may be fitting when the family wishes to emphasise God's compassion throughout the journey of illness.

Its language is steady and hopeful.

A Final Thought When Choosing

When selecting a Psalm after long illness, consider:

- Do you wish to acknowledge perseverance and endurance?
- Would language centred on rest feel appropriate?
- Does the Psalm offer calm reassurance when spoken aloud?

In these circumstances, psalms that speak of trust and peace often provide the greatest comfort.

Second Readings (New Testament Letters)

The Second Reading is usually taken from the New Testament letters or the Book of Revelation. It follows the Psalm and prepares the way for the Gospel.

In many Catholic and Christian funerals, this reading speaks directly of faith, resurrection, endurance and eternal life. While the First Reading often reflects the life that was lived, the Second Reading frequently centres on Christian hope.

The passages listed here are among the most commonly chosen. Your parish may offer additional approved options.

For a Mother

When selecting a Second Reading for a mother, families often look for passages that speak of love, endurance and the promise of eternal life. These readings frequently emphasise hope beyond sorrow.

Below are New Testament readings that may feel especially appropriate.

Revelation 21:1–5

"Then I saw a new heaven and a new earth... prepared as a bride beautifully dressed..."

This passage presents death not as an ending, but as a homecoming. Its imagery of a new heaven and the wiping away of tears can feel especially comforting when remembering a mother whose faith shaped her life.

It may be chosen when the focus is on reunion, promise and eternal peace.

Romans 8:35–39

"Nothing can separate us from the love of God."

This passage speaks of unwavering love that endures beyond suffering and death. It may feel especially meaningful when a mother's love reflected steadfast faith.

Its tone is confident and reassuring.

1 Corinthians 13:1–13

"Love is patient, love is kind."

Often chosen when love was central to a mother's life, this passage reflects enduring charity and faith. It may be especially appropriate when the family wishes to emphasise the lasting impact of love.

Because it is widely known, it can feel familiar and comforting.

2 Timothy 4:6–8

"I have fought the good fight, I have finished the race."

This reading may be fitting when a mother endured illness or hardship with perseverance. It reflects completion and faithfulness.

It carries dignity without heaviness.

A Final Thought When Choosing

When selecting a Second Reading for a mother, consider:

- Do you wish to emphasise eternal reunion?
- Was her life marked by enduring love?

- Would a focus on faithfulness feel appropriate?

These readings speak clearly of Christian hope and promise.

For a Father

When selecting a Second Reading for a father, families often look for passages that reflect faithfulness, perseverance and the promise of eternal life. These readings frequently emphasise endurance and hope beyond hardship.

Below are New Testament readings that may feel especially appropriate.

2 Timothy 4:6–8

"I have fought the good fight, I have finished the race."

This passage reflects completion and faithfulness. It may be especially meaningful when remembering a father who endured illness or responsibility with steady perseverance.

It carries dignity without heaviness.

Romans 8:35–39

"Nothing can separate us from the love of God."

This reading speaks of unwavering love and security in Christ. It may feel especially appropriate when faith was central to a father's life.

Its tone is confident and reassuring.

1 Corinthians 15:20–23

"Christ has been raised from the dead."

This passage centres directly on resurrection and hope. It may be chosen when the focus is on Christian belief in life beyond death.

It is clear, doctrinal and steady.

Philippians 3:20–21

"Our citizenship is in heaven."
This reading reflects belonging beyond this world. It may be fitting when the family wishes to emphasise eternal hope and promise.

Its tone is reflective and forward-looking.

A Final Thought When Choosing

When selecting a Second Reading for a father, consider:

- Was his life marked by endurance and perseverance?
- Do you wish to emphasise resurrection and eternal promise?
- Would a confident tone of hope feel appropriate?

These readings speak clearly of faithfulness and Christian assurance.

For an Adult Woman

When selecting a Second Reading for an adult woman, families often look for passages that reflect love, faithfulness and the promise of eternal life. These readings frequently emphasise hope, identity in Christ and the enduring nature of love.

Below are New Testament readings that may feel especially appropriate.

Romans 8:35–39

"Nothing can separate us from the love of God."
This passage speaks of unwavering love that endures beyond suffering and death. It may be especially meaningful when remembering a woman whose faith or love shaped her life.

Its tone is confident and reassuring.

1 Corinthians 13:1–13

"Love is patient, love is kind."

Often chosen when love and generosity were central to her life, this passage reflects enduring charity and faith. It may feel especially appropriate when the family wishes to emphasise the lasting impact of love.

Because it is widely known, it can feel familiar and comforting.

Revelation 21:3–4

"He will wipe every tear from their eyes."

Selected verses from this passage may be chosen when the focus is on reunion and the promise of a place where sorrow is no more.

It carries a tone of hope and completion.

2 Corinthians 5:1

"We have a building from God, an eternal house in heaven."

This reading reflects confidence in life beyond earthly limitations. It may feel fitting when the family wishes to emphasise eternal dwelling and belonging.

Its tone is calm and assured.

A Final Thought When Choosing

When selecting a Second Reading for an adult woman, consider:

- Was love central to her life and relationships?
- Do you wish to emphasise reunion and eternal promise?
- Would a tone of confident hope feel most appropriate?

These readings speak clearly of faith, love and Christian assurance.

For an Adult Man

When selecting a Second Reading for an adult man, families often look for passages that reflect perseverance, faithfulness and the promise of eternal life. These readings frequently speak of endurance and the certainty of Christian hope.

Below are New Testament readings that may feel especially appropriate.

2 Timothy 4:6–8

"I have fought the good fight, I have finished the race."
This passage reflects completion and faithful endurance. It may be especially meaningful when remembering a man who carried responsibility with steadiness or faced illness with resilience.

Its tone is dignified and assured.

Romans 14:7–9

"Whether we live or die, we belong to the Lord."
This reading centres on belonging and faith in Christ beyond earthly life. It may feel especially appropriate when faith was visible in his daily life.

Its language is clear and confident.

1 Corinthians 15:51–57

"Death has been swallowed up in victory."
This passage speaks directly of resurrection and triumph over death. It may be chosen when the focus is firmly on Christian belief in eternal life.

It should be selected thoughtfully, as its tone is strong and declarative.

Philippians 1:21–23

"To live is Christ and to die is gain."

This reading reflects confidence in eternal hope. It may feel fitting when the family wishes to emphasise faith and assurance.

Its tone is reflective yet firm.

A Final Thought When Choosing

When selecting a Second Reading for an adult man, consider:

- Was his life marked by perseverance and responsibility?
- Do you wish to emphasise belonging and faith?
- Would a confident tone of resurrection feel appropriate?

These readings speak clearly of endurance and Christian hope.

For a Teenager

When selecting a Second Reading for a teenager, families often look for passages that speak of identity, love and hope beyond sorrow. In circumstances of early loss, clarity and reassurance are usually more appropriate than complexity.

These readings focus on belonging to God and the enduring nature of love.

Below are New Testament readings that may feel especially appropriate.

Romans 8:38–39

"Nothing can separate us from the love of God."

This passage affirms that love endures beyond suffering and death. It may feel especially meaningful when remembering a young person whose life was marked by strong relationships and deep connection.

Its tone is steady and reassuring.

1 Corinthians 13:4–8

"Love never fails."

Selected verses from this passage may be chosen when the focus is on the lasting impact of love. It is widely known and often brings comfort through familiarity.

Its tone is gentle and reflective.

Revelation 21:3–4

"He will wipe every tear from their eyes."

These verses may be especially comforting in times of early loss. They speak of a place where sorrow is no more and offer quiet reassurance of eternal peace.

Its tone is hopeful and tender.

1 John 3:1–2

"See what great love the Father has lavished on us."

This reading reflects identity and belonging in God's love. It may feel especially meaningful when remembering a young person whose life was filled with promise.

Its language is simple and affirming.

A Final Thought When Choosing

When selecting a Second Reading for a teenager, consider:

- Would reassurance about enduring love feel most helpful?
- Do you prefer simple and familiar language?

- Does the reading reflect hope without heaviness?

In circumstances of early loss, steady and compassionate words often bring the greatest comfort.

For a Child

When selecting a Second Reading for a child, families often look for passages that speak of love, belonging and God's gentle care. In these circumstances, simplicity and clarity are especially important.

These readings focus less on explanation and more on reassurance and hope.

Below are New Testament readings that may feel especially appropriate.

Romans 8:38–39

"Nothing can separate us from the love of God."

This passage speaks of love that endures beyond all circumstances. It may feel especially comforting when the focus is on reassurance for those gathered.

Its tone is calm and steady.

1 John 3:1

"See what great love the Father has lavished on us."

This short reading reflects identity and belonging in God's love. It may be especially meaningful when remembering a child whose life was deeply cherished.

Its language is gentle and affirming.

Revelation 21:4

"He will wipe every tear from their eyes."

This verse may be chosen when families wish to emphasise comfort and peace. It speaks directly to sorrow without explanation.

Its tone is tender and hopeful.

Matthew 18:5

"Whoever welcomes one such child in my name welcomes me."

Although taken from the Gospels, this short verse is sometimes referenced in Christian services. It reflects the dignity and value of a child's life.

It should be chosen when simplicity is preferred.

A Final Thought When Choosing

When selecting a Second Reading for a child, consider:

- Would short and gentle words feel most appropriate?
- Is reassurance more helpful than reflection?
- Does the reading offer comfort without complexity?

In these circumstances, calm and affirming language often brings the greatest peace.

For a Baby or Infant

When selecting a Second Reading for a baby or infant, simplicity is especially important. Families are often overwhelmed, and shorter passages may feel more appropriate.

These readings focus on love, belonging and the promise of peace.

Below are New Testament readings that may feel fitting in these circumstances.

Romans 8:38–39

"Nothing can separate us from the love of God."

This passage affirms that love endures beyond all circumstances. It may feel especially reassuring when words are difficult to find.

Its tone is steady and comforting.

Revelation 21:4

"He will wipe every tear from their eyes."

This brief verse speaks directly of comfort and peace. It may be chosen when families wish to focus on tenderness rather than explanation.

Its language is simple and hopeful.

1 John 4:7–8

"Let us love one another, for love comes from God."

Selected verses from this passage may be chosen when the emphasis is on the love that surrounded the child's life, however brief.

Its tone is gentle and affirming.

A Final Thought When Choosing

When selecting a Second Reading for a baby or infant, shorter passages are often most appropriate.

Choose language that feels calm and reassuring when spoken aloud. In these circumstances, simple words of love and promise often bring the greatest comfort.

For Sudden or Unexpected Loss

When death comes suddenly, families are often searching for steadiness rather than interpretation. The Second Reading can offer reassurance of God's presence and the certainty of Christian hope, without attempting to explain what cannot be explained.

Below are New Testament readings that may feel appropriate when loss was unexpected.

Romans 8:35–39

"Nothing can separate us from the love of God."

This passage speaks of enduring love that remains constant through all circumstances. It may be especially meaningful when the focus is on reassurance rather than reasoning.

Its tone is confident and steady.

1 Thessalonians 4:13–14

"Do not grieve as others do who have no hope."

This reading speaks directly of sorrow while affirming Christian hope. It acknowledges grief without diminishing it.

It should be chosen thoughtfully, ensuring the tone suits the family's circumstances.

Revelation 21:3–4

"He will wipe every tear from their eyes."

These verses offer reassurance of comfort and peace beyond earthly sorrow. They may feel especially steady when shock is still present.

Its tone is hopeful and tender.

2 Corinthians 5:1

"We have a building from God, an eternal house in heaven."

This passage reflects confidence in eternal dwelling and belonging. It may be meaningful when the focus is on promise rather than explanation.

Its tone is calm and assured.

A Final Thought When Choosing

When selecting a Second Reading after sudden loss, consider:

- Would reassurance about enduring love feel most appropriate?
- Does the reading acknowledge sorrow without overwhelming it?
- Does it offer steady hope rather than interpretation?

In times of shock, clear and confident language of promise often brings the greatest comfort.

For Long Illness

When death follows a period of illness, families often reflect on perseverance, care and quiet endurance. In these circumstances, the Second Reading can gently acknowledge faithfulness while turning the focus toward rest and eternal promise.

Below are New Testament readings that may feel especially appropriate when illness has been part of the journey.

2 Timothy 4:6–8

"I have fought the good fight, I have finished the race."

This passage reflects completion and faithful endurance. It may be especially meaningful when remembering someone who faced illness with courage and dignity.

Its tone is resolute and hopeful.

2 Corinthians 4:16–18

"Therefore we do not lose heart."

This reading speaks of perseverance and renewal beyond visible suffering. It may feel fitting when the family wishes to acknowledge hardship while affirming eternal perspective.

Its tone is reflective and steady.

Philippians 3:20–21

"Our citizenship is in heaven."

This passage centres on belonging beyond earthly limitations. It may be chosen when the focus is on promise and transformation.

Its tone is calm and forward-looking.

Revelation 21:4

"He will wipe every tear from their eyes."

This verse may be especially meaningful after prolonged illness. It speaks directly of comfort and the end of suffering.

Its language is simple and reassuring.

A Final Thought When Choosing

When selecting a Second Reading after long illness, consider:

- Do you wish to emphasise endurance and completion?
- Would language centred on rest feel appropriate?
- Does the reading offer quiet assurance rather than intensity?

In these circumstances, passages that speak of perseverance and peace often provide the greatest comfort.

Gospel Readings

The Gospel reading is the central proclamation within a Catholic or Christian funeral service. In Catholic liturgy, it is proclaimed by the priest or deacon and is traditionally selected by the celebrant, although families may express a preference.

The Gospel focuses directly on the words and promise of Christ. While the First and Second Readings often reflect the life that was lived and the hope of eternal life, the Gospel brings the voice of Christ to the centre of the service.

The passages listed here are among those commonly chosen for funerals. Your parish or minister will guide the final selection.

For a Mother

When considering a Gospel reading for a mother, families often look for passages that reflect love, reassurance and the promise of eternal homecoming.

Below are Gospel passages that may feel especially appropriate.

John 14:1–6

"Do not let your hearts be troubled... In my Father's house there are many rooms."

This passage is one of the most frequently chosen Gospel readings for funerals. It speaks of preparation, belonging and reunion.

It may be especially meaningful when remembering a mother whose faith offered comfort and steadiness to her family.

John 11:21–27

"I am the resurrection and the life."
Spoken at the raising of Lazarus, this passage centres directly on Christ's promise of life beyond death. It may be chosen when the focus is firmly on resurrection and Christian hope.

Its tone is strong and confident.

Luke 23:39–43

"Today you will be with me in paradise."
This brief passage reflects mercy and assurance. It may feel appropriate when the family wishes to emphasise God's compassion and welcome.

Its language is simple and direct.

Matthew 11:28–30

"Come to me, all you who are weary."
This reading speaks of rest and relief from burden. It may be especially meaningful when a mother endured illness or long responsibility with quiet faith.

Its tone is gentle and reassuring.

A Final Thought When Choosing

When considering a Gospel for a mother, reflect on:

- Do you wish to emphasise reunion and homecoming?
- Would reassurance and comfort feel most appropriate?
- Does the passage reflect the tone of hope you wish to express?

The Gospel brings the words of Christ to the centre of the service, and its selection shapes the heart of the message.

For a Father

When considering a Gospel reading for a father, families often look for passages that reflect trust, faithfulness and the promise of eternal life.

Below are Gospel passages that may feel especially appropriate.

John 14:1–6

"Do not let your hearts be troubled."

This passage speaks of preparation and belonging. It may be especially meaningful when remembering a father who provided steadiness and reassurance to his family.

Its tone is calm and confident.

John 11:25–26

"I am the resurrection and the life."

This declaration of Christ's promise is frequently chosen at funerals. It may be fitting when the focus is firmly on Christian hope and resurrection.

Its language is clear and assured.

Luke 24:13–35

"The road to Emmaus."

This passage reflects companionship and recognition of Christ's presence even in sorrow. It may feel appropriate when the family wishes to acknowledge grief while affirming hope.

It is reflective and narrative in tone.

Matthew 25:21

"Well done, good and faithful servant."

Selected verses from this passage may be chosen when remembering a life of service and commitment. It may feel especially fitting when faithfulness defined his life.

Its tone is affirming and dignified.

A Final Thought When Choosing

When considering a Gospel for a father, reflect on:

- Was faith central to his life?
- Do you wish to emphasise resurrection and promise?
- Would a tone of affirmation feel appropriate?

The Gospel shapes the central message of the service and should feel aligned with both faith and remembrance.

For an Adult Woman

When considering a Gospel reading for an adult woman, families often look for passages that reflect compassion, belonging and the promise of eternal life. The Gospel places the words of Christ at the centre of the service, offering both reassurance and hope.

Below are Gospel passages that may feel especially appropriate.

John 14:1–6

"Do not let your hearts be troubled... In my Father's house there are many rooms."

This passage speaks of preparation and eternal belonging. It may feel especially meaningful when remembering a woman whose faith provided comfort and steadiness to others.

Its tone is reassuring and hopeful.

John 11:21–27

"I am the resurrection and the life."

Spoken to Martha at the death of her brother, this passage reflects both grief and faith. It may be especially appropriate when the family wishes to emphasise trust in Christ's promise.

Its tone is confident yet compassionate.

Luke 10:38–42

"Martha and Mary."

This passage reflects devotion and attentiveness to Christ. It may feel fitting when remembering a woman whose faith, hospitality or service were central to her life.

Its tone is reflective and personal.

Matthew 5:1–12

"The Beatitudes."

This reading reflects blessing, mercy and promise. It may be especially meaningful when a woman's life was marked by gentleness, compassion or perseverance.

Its tone is contemplative and affirming.

A Final Thought When Choosing

When considering a Gospel for an adult woman, reflect on:

- Do you wish to emphasise reassurance or blessing?
- Was compassion or devotion central to her life?

- Does the passage reflect both faith and hope?

The Gospel should feel aligned with the life remembered while remaining centred on Christ's promise.

For an Adult Man

When considering a Gospel reading for an adult man, families often look for passages that reflect faithfulness, service and the promise of eternal life. The Gospel brings the words of Christ to the centre of the service and shapes its core message.

Below are Gospel passages that may feel especially appropriate.

John 14:1–6

"Do not let your hearts be troubled."

This passage speaks of preparation and eternal dwelling. It may feel especially fitting when remembering a man who offered steadiness and reassurance to his family.

Its tone is calm and confident.

John 11:25–26

"I am the resurrection and the life."

This declaration of Christ's promise is frequently chosen at funerals. It centres directly on hope and eternal life.

Its language is clear and assured.

Matthew 25:21

"Well done, good and faithful servant."

Selected verses from this passage may be chosen when remembering a life of service and responsibility. It may feel especially meaningful when faithfulness defined his character.

Its tone is affirming and dignified.

Luke 24:13–35

"The road to Emmaus."

This narrative reflects Christ's presence in times of sorrow and confusion. It may be especially appropriate when the family wishes to acknowledge grief while affirming that faith continues through it.

Its tone is reflective and steady.

A Final Thought When Choosing

When considering a Gospel for an adult man, reflect on:

- Was service or faithfulness central to his life?
- Do you wish to emphasise resurrection and promise?
- Does the passage align with the tone of hope you wish to create?

The Gospel shapes the heart of the service and should feel both reverent and personal.

For a Teenager

When considering a Gospel reading for a teenager, families often look for passages that reflect belonging, compassion and hope beyond sorrow. In circumstances of early loss, simplicity and clarity are especially important.

The Gospel should offer reassurance without overwhelming explanation. Below are Gospel passages that may feel especially appropriate.

John 14:1–6

"Do not let your hearts be troubled."

This passage speaks of preparation and belonging. It may be especially meaningful when shock is still present and reassurance is needed.

Its tone is calm and steady.

John 11:32–36

"Jesus wept."

These verses acknowledge sorrow directly. They reflect that grief itself is not without faith.

It may be chosen when the family wishes to affirm that loss and belief coexist.

Matthew 5:3–10

"Blessed are those who mourn."

Selected verses from the Beatitudes may be especially meaningful when comfort and promise are central themes.

Its tone is contemplative and reassuring.

Luke 23:39–43

"Today you will be with me in paradise."

This brief passage reflects mercy and welcome. It may feel appropriate when the focus is on assurance and peace.

Its language is simple and direct.

A Final Thought When Choosing

When considering a Gospel for a teenager, reflect on:

- Would reassurance feel most helpful?
- Does the passage acknowledge sorrow without explanation?
- Does it centre on Christ's promise rather than circumstance?

In circumstances of early loss, steady and compassionate words often speak most clearly.

For a Child

When considering a Gospel reading for a child, families often look for passages that reflect welcome, tenderness and belonging. In these circumstances, simplicity and clarity are especially important.

The Gospel should centre on Christ's compassion and care.

Below are Gospel passages that may feel especially appropriate.

Matthew 19:13–14

"Let the little children come to me."

This passage reflects Christ's welcome and blessing of children. It may feel especially meaningful when remembering a child whose life was deeply cherished.

Its tone is gentle and affirming.

John 14:1–6

"Do not let your hearts be troubled."

This passage offers reassurance and promise. It may be chosen when the family wishes to centre the service on belonging and eternal home.

Its language is calm and steady.

John 11:35

"Jesus wept."

This brief verse acknowledges sorrow without explanation. It may be especially meaningful when the family wishes to affirm that grief is not contrary to faith.

Its simplicity can be deeply moving.

Luke 18:16

"The kingdom of God belongs to such as these."

This passage reflects dignity and value in the life of a child. It may feel appropriate when the focus is on innocence and welcome.

Its tone is clear and hopeful.

A Final Thought When Choosing

When considering a Gospel for a child, reflect on:

- Would a passage centred on Christ's welcome feel most appropriate?
- Does the language feel gentle when spoken aloud?
- Does the reading offer reassurance without complexity?

In these moments, simple words of compassion and belonging often bring the greatest comfort.

For a Baby or Infant

When considering a Gospel reading for a baby or infant, simplicity is especially important. Families are often overwhelmed, and shorter passages may feel more appropriate.

The Gospel should centre on Christ's welcome and compassion.

Below are Gospel passages that may feel fitting in these circumstances.

Matthew 19:14

"Let the little children come to me."

This passage reflects Christ's welcome and blessing. It may feel especially meaningful when the focus is on tenderness and belonging.

Its language is simple and reassuring.

Luke 18:16

"The kingdom of God belongs to such as these."

This verse reflects dignity and value. It may be chosen when families wish to emphasise that the child is welcomed and cherished.

Its tone is calm and affirming.

John 14:1–3

"In my Father's house there are many rooms."

Selected verses from this passage may be chosen when the focus is on belonging and eternal dwelling.

Its language is steady and hopeful.

A Final Thought When Choosing

When considering a Gospel for a baby or infant, shorter passages are often most appropriate.

Choose words that feel gentle and clear when proclaimed. In these circumstances, Christ's welcome and promise often provide the greatest reassurance.

For Sudden or Unexpected Loss

When death comes suddenly, families are often searching for steadiness rather than explanation. The Gospel should offer reassurance through the words of Christ, without attempting to interpret what cannot be understood.

Below are Gospel passages that may feel especially appropriate when loss was unexpected.

John 14:1–6

"Do not let your hearts be troubled."
This passage offers calm reassurance and speaks of preparation and belonging. It may be especially meaningful when shock is still present and steady language is needed.

Its tone is composed and hopeful.

John 11:32–36

"Jesus wept."
These verses acknowledge sorrow directly. They reflect that grief itself is not without faith.

It may be chosen when the family wishes to affirm that loss and belief can coexist.

Luke 24:13–35

"The road to Emmaus."

This narrative reflects Christ's presence even when understanding feels distant. It may feel appropriate when the family wishes to acknowledge confusion and grief while affirming hope.

Its tone is reflective and steady.

Matthew 11:28

"Come to me, all you who are weary."

This brief invitation speaks of rest and relief. It may feel especially fitting when the family seeks comfort without explanation.

Its language is gentle and direct.

A Final Thought When Choosing

When considering a Gospel after sudden loss, reflect on:

- Would reassurance feel more helpful than interpretation?
- Does the passage acknowledge sorrow without overwhelming it?
- Does it centre on Christ's presence and promise?

In times of shock, steady and compassionate words often bring the greatest comfort.

For Long Illness

When death follows a period of illness, families often reflect on endurance, care and quiet perseverance. In these circumstances, the Gospel can gently acknowledge that journey while turning the focus toward rest and eternal promise.

Below are Gospel passages that may feel especially appropriate when illness has been part of the story.

Matthew 11:28–30

"Come to me, all you who are weary."

This passage speaks directly of rest after burden. It may be especially meaningful when a long illness has brought exhaustion and the family wishes to emphasise peace.

Its tone is gentle and reassuring.

John 14:1–6

"In my Father's house there are many rooms."

This reading centres on preparation and belonging. It may feel fitting when the focus is on homecoming after a long journey.

Its language is steady and hopeful.

John 11:25–26

"I am the resurrection and the life."

This declaration of Christ's promise may be chosen when the emphasis is on faith and eternal life beyond suffering.

Its tone is confident and assured.

Luke 23:43

"Today you will be with me in paradise."

This brief assurance may feel especially appropriate when the family wishes to centre on mercy and welcome.

Its language is simple and direct.

A Final Thought When Choosing

When considering a Gospel after long illness, reflect on:

- Do you wish to emphasise rest and peace?
- Would language centred on homecoming feel appropriate?
- Does the passage offer calm reassurance when proclaimed?

In these circumstances, Gospel readings that speak of invitation and promise often provide the greatest comfort.

Prayers of the Faithful (Intercessions)

The Prayers of the Faithful, also known as the Intercessions, follow the Gospel and homily in a Catholic funeral Mass. These prayers allow the congregation to pray for the person who has died, for their family, and for the wider community.

In many parishes, families are invited to prepare these prayers or to suggest intentions that reflect the life of the deceased.

The structure is usually simple:

- A prayer for the person who has died
- A prayer for family and friends
- A prayer for those who are grieving
- A prayer for the sick or those in need
- A prayer for the Church and the wider world

Each prayer is brief and followed by a response such as:

Lord, hear our prayer.

The examples below may be used as written or adapted to suit your circumstances.

For a Mother

1. For (Name), that she may be welcomed into the peace of Christ and share in the fullness of eternal life.

Lord, hear our prayer.

2. For her children and family, that they may be comforted in their grief and strengthened by the faith she shared with them.

Lord, hear our prayer.

3. For all mothers, especially those who carry heavy responsibility, that they may find support and encouragement in their vocation.

Lord, hear our prayer.

4. For those who are grieving the loss of a mother, that they may find reassurance in God's promise of eternal life.

Lord, hear our prayer.

5. For all who are sick or elderly, that they may know Christ's presence and peace.

Lord, hear our prayer.

6. For the Church and for all gathered here, that we may live with hope in the resurrection.

Lord, hear our prayer.

For a Father

1. For (Name), that he may be welcomed into the peace of Christ and share in the joy of eternal life.

Lord, hear our prayer.

2. For his family and friends, that they may be comforted in their grief and strengthened by the faith and example he shared with them.

Lord, hear our prayer.

3. For fathers and those who carry responsibility for others, that they may find guidance and support in their vocation.

Lord, hear our prayer.

4. For all who are grieving the loss of a father, that they may find reassurance in God's promise of resurrection.

Lord, hear our prayer.

5. For those who are ill or burdened, that they may know Christ's compassion and peace.

Lord, hear our prayer.

6. For the Church and for all gathered here, that we may live in hope and trust in God's mercy.

Lord, hear our prayer.

For an Adult Woman

1. For (Name), that she may be welcomed into the light and peace of Christ and share in eternal life.

Lord, hear our prayer.

2. For her family and friends, that they may be comforted in their grief and strengthened by the memories they carry.

Lord, hear our prayer.

3. For all women who serve, lead and care for others, that they may find encouragement and support in their daily lives.

Lord, hear our prayer.

4. For those who feel the weight of loss today, that they may know God's closeness and compassion.

Lord, hear our prayer.

5. For those who are sick or in need of support, that they may experience Christ's healing presence.

Lord, hear our prayer.

6. For the Church and for all gathered here, that we may live with hope in the promise of resurrection.

Lord, hear our prayer.

For an Adult Man

1. For (Name), that he may be welcomed into the peace and joy of Christ and share in eternal life.

Lord, hear our prayer.

2. For his family and friends, that they may be comforted in their grief and strengthened by the example he set in his life.

Lord, hear our prayer.

3. For all who carry responsibility for others, that they may be guided by wisdom and supported in their work and service.

Lord, hear our prayer.

4. For those who are mourning today, that they may find reassurance in God's enduring love.

Lord, hear our prayer.

5. For the sick, the elderly and those who feel alone, that they may know Christ's presence and peace.

Lord, hear our prayer.

6. For the Church and for all gathered here, that we may remain steadfast in faith and hope.

Lord, hear our prayer.

For a Teenager

1. For (Name), that he/she may be welcomed into the loving presence of Christ and share in the joy of eternal life.

Lord, hear our prayer.

2. For parents, family and friends who grieve a life taken too soon, that they may be strengthened and comforted in the days ahead.

Lord, hear our prayer.

3. For young people everywhere, that they may be supported, protected and guided in hope.

Lord, hear our prayer.

4. For friends and classmates who struggle with shock and sadness, that they may find reassurance in God's love.

Lord, hear our prayer.

5. For all who feel lost or overwhelmed by grief, that they may know Christ's closeness and compassion.

Lord, hear our prayer.

6. For the Church and for this community, that we may hold one another in care and live in hope of resurrection.

Lord, hear our prayer.

For a Child

1. For (Name), that he/she may be welcomed into the loving arms of Christ and share in eternal peace.

Lord, hear our prayer.

2. For parents and family who grieve deeply today, that they may be comforted and supported in their sorrow.

Lord, hear our prayer.

3. For brothers, sisters and friends, that they may be reassured and cared for in the days ahead.

Lord, hear our prayer.

4. For all children, that they may grow in safety, love and protection.

Lord, hear our prayer.

5. For those who struggle to understand this loss, that they may find gentle reassurance in God's presence.

Lord, hear our prayer.

6. For our community and the Church, that we may remain united in faith and hope.

Lord, hear our prayer.

For a Baby or Infant

1. For (Name), that he/she may be welcomed into the peace and love of Christ.
Lord, hear our prayer.

2. For parents and family who carry deep sorrow, that they may be held and comforted in their grief.
Lord, hear our prayer.

3. For all families who have experienced the loss of a child, that they may find support and compassion.
Lord, hear our prayer.

4. For those who feel overwhelmed or without words, that they may know God's closeness.
Lord, hear our prayer.

5. For our community and the Church, that we may respond with tenderness and care.
Lord, hear our prayer.

For Sudden or Unexpected Loss

1. For (Name), that he/she may be welcomed into the peace of Christ and share in eternal life.
Lord, hear our prayer.

2. For family and friends who are shocked and grieving, that they may be strengthened and supported in the days ahead.
Lord, hear our prayer.

3. For those who struggle with unanswered questions, that they may find steadiness in God's presence.
Lord, hear our prayer.

4. For all who carry sudden loss in their hearts, that they may know compassion and understanding.
Lord, hear our prayer.

5. For those who feel overwhelmed by grief, that they may experience

Christ's closeness.

Lord, hear our prayer.

6. For our community and the Church, that we may respond with care and remain firm in hope.

Lord, hear our prayer.

For Long Illness

1. For (Name), that after a time of illness and struggle, he/she may now rest in the peace and presence of Christ.

Lord, hear our prayer.

2. For family members and carers who gave support and love throughout this journey, that they may be strengthened and comforted.

Lord, hear our prayer.

3. For all who are living with illness, that they may know courage, relief from suffering and the support of those around them.

Lord, hear our prayer.

4. For medical staff and caregivers, that their work may be guided by compassion and wisdom.

Lord, hear our prayer.

5. For those who feel weary in body or spirit, that they may find renewal and hope.

Lord, hear our prayer.

6. For our community and the Church, that we may remain faithful and trust in the promise of eternal life.

Lord, hear our prayer.

Music and Hymns

Music plays a significant role in a Catholic or Christian funeral service. It allows the congregation to pray together and often carries deep emotional meaning.

In a Catholic funeral Mass, music is chosen carefully to reflect faith and hope in Christ. Parishes usually provide guidance and may require that hymns be liturgically appropriate. Some songs that hold personal meaning may be better suited for before or after the Mass, or at the graveside.

The selections below include commonly chosen hymns as well as reflective songs that families sometimes consider. Your parish or minister will guide what is permitted within the service.

For a Mother

When selecting music for a mother's funeral, families often look for hymns that reflect love, faith and reassurance. Because music is prayed as well as sung, familiar hymns can bring comfort to those gathered.

Commonly Chosen Hymns

- **Amazing Grace**
- A widely known hymn that speaks of redemption and hope. Its familiarity often brings comfort to congregations of all ages.
- **Be Not Afraid**

- Based on Scripture, this hymn reflects reassurance and trust in God's presence.
- **Here I Am, Lord**
- Often chosen when faith and service were central to her life.
- **On Eagle's Wings**
- A gentle and reassuring hymn that speaks of protection and rest.
- **Hail Mary, Gentle Woman**
- Sometimes chosen in Catholic funerals, especially when Marian devotion was important.

Reflective Songs (Where Permitted)

Some families consider reflective songs that hold personal meaning. These are often more appropriate before or after the Mass.

- **Ave Maria**
- Often sung during Communion or as a reflection.
- **The Prayer**
- Sometimes chosen outside the formal liturgy when personal meaning is central.

Families should confirm with their parish what is appropriate within the Mass itself.

For a Father

When selecting music for a father's funeral, families often look for hymns that reflect faith, strength and reassurance. Familiar hymns can help the congregation participate confidently in prayer.

Commonly Chosen Hymns

- **Amazing Grace**
- Frequently chosen for its message of redemption and enduring hope.
- **How Great Thou Art**
- A strong and confident hymn reflecting praise and trust in God.
- **Be Not Afraid**
- Offers reassurance and comfort in times of sorrow.
- **I Am the Bread of Life**
- Often sung during Communion, reflecting faith in eternal life.
- **On Eagle's Wings**
- A steady and prayerful hymn centred on protection and peace.

Reflective Songs (Where Permitted)

Some families choose a piece of music that held personal meaning. These are usually more appropriate outside the formal liturgy.

- **My Way**
- Sometimes chosen as a reflection after Mass or at the graveside.
- **The Lord's Prayer**
- Often sung within liturgical guidelines, depending on parish practice.

Always confirm with your parish or celebrant what is permitted within the Mass.

For an Adult Woman

When selecting music for an adult woman's funeral, families often look for hymns that reflect faith, dignity and reassurance. Music that is familiar and prayerful can help the congregation participate with confidence.

Commonly Chosen Hymns

- **Amazing Grace**
- A hymn of hope and redemption that is widely known and often comforting.
- **Be Not Afraid**
- Reflects trust in God's presence and reassurance in sorrow.
- **Here I Am, Lord**
- Often chosen when service, generosity or faith were central to her life.
- **On Eagle's Wings**
- A gentle and prayerful hymn centred on protection and peace.
- **The King of Love My Shepherd Is**
- Based on Psalm 23, this hymn reflects guidance and enduring care.

Reflective Songs (Where Permitted)

Some families choose a song that held personal meaning. These are often more appropriate before or after the Mass.

- **Ave Maria**
- Frequently sung as a reflective piece, especially where Marian devotion was meaningful.
- **You Raise Me Up**
- Sometimes chosen for its message of support and strength, typically outside the formal liturgy.

Always confirm with your parish or minister what is appropriate within the service.

For an Adult Man

When selecting music for an adult man's funeral, families often look for hymns that reflect faith, strength and trust in God's promise. Familiar and well-known hymns can help the congregation participate confidently in prayer.

Commonly Chosen Hymns

- **How Great Thou Art**
- A strong and reverent hymn expressing praise and confidence in God.
- **Amazing Grace**
- Frequently chosen for its message of redemption and enduring hope.
- **Be Not Afraid**
- Reflects reassurance and trust during sorrow.
- **I Am the Bread of Life**
- Often sung during Communion, centred on faith in eternal life.
- **The Old Rugged Cross**
- Sometimes chosen in Christian services where the Cross was central to faith expression.

Reflective Songs (Where Permitted)

Some families choose a song that reflects personality or personal meaning. These are usually more appropriate before or after the Mass, or at the graveside.

- **My Way**
- Often selected as a tribute piece outside the formal liturgy.
- **Time to Say Goodbye**
- Sometimes chosen as a reflective piece, typically outside the Mass.

Always confirm with your parish or celebrant what is permitted within the service.

For a Teenager

When selecting music for a teenager's funeral, families often look for hymns that reflect hope, reassurance and belonging. Familiar hymns can provide stability when emotions are overwhelming.

Commonly Chosen Hymns

- **Be Not Afraid**
- Offers reassurance and trust in God's presence.
- **On Eagle's Wings**
- A gentle and prayerful hymn centred on protection and peace.
- **Amazing Grace**
- Widely known and often comforting across generations.
- **Here I Am, Lord**
- Reflects faith and response, often chosen when hope is central.

Reflective Songs (Where Permitted)

Families may wish to include a song that held personal meaning for the young person. These are often more appropriate before or after the Mass.

- **You Raise Me Up**
- Sometimes chosen for its message of support and strength.
- **I Can Only Imagine**
- A Christian contemporary song reflecting hope in heaven, typically used outside the formal liturgy.

Parish guidelines should always be confirmed before finalising selections.

For a Child

When selecting music for a child's funeral, families often look for hymns that are gentle, familiar and reassuring. Simple melodies can help the congregation participate when emotions are close to the surface.

Commonly Chosen Hymns

- **Jesus Loves Me**
- A simple and widely recognised hymn that reflects love and belonging.
- **Amazing Grace**
- Frequently chosen for its message of hope and redemption.
- **On Eagle's Wings**
- A gentle hymn centred on protection and peace.
- **Be Not Afraid**
- Offers reassurance in times of sorrow.
- **The Lord Is My Shepherd**
- Often sung in settings appropriate for Catholic liturgy.

Reflective Music (Where Permitted)

Some families may choose a soft instrumental piece or a simple reflective song before or after the Mass.

Always confirm with your parish what is permitted within the liturgy itself.

For a Baby or Infant

When selecting music for a baby or infant's funeral, simplicity and gentleness are especially important. Soft, familiar hymns can provide comfort when words feel difficult.

Commonly Chosen Hymns

- **Jesus Loves Me**
- A simple and reassuring hymn reflecting love and belonging.
- **Amazing Grace**
- Frequently chosen for its familiar and comforting message.
- **On Eagle's Wings**
- A gentle hymn centred on protection and peace.
- **The Lord Is My Shepherd**
- Often sung in settings appropriate for Catholic liturgy.

Instrumental or Reflective Music (Where Permitted)

Some families choose a soft instrumental piece before or after the Mass. These selections are usually best placed outside the formal liturgy.

Parish approval should always be confirmed when including non-liturgical music.

For Sudden or Unexpected Loss

When death comes suddenly, familiar hymns can provide stability and reassurance. In moments of shock, music that is widely known and easy to sing often feels most appropriate.

Commonly Chosen Hymns

- **Be Not Afraid**
- Offers reassurance and trust in God's presence during uncertainty.
- **On Eagle's Wings**
- A gentle and steady hymn centred on protection and peace.
- **Amazing Grace**
- Frequently chosen for its message of hope beyond sorrow.

- **The Lord Is My Shepherd**
  - A familiar and grounding choice, often used in Catholic liturgy.

Reflective Music (Where Permitted)

In cases of sudden loss, families sometimes choose a quiet instrumental piece before or after the Mass to allow space for reflection.

Parish guidance should always be sought when including non-liturgical music.

For Long Illness

When death follows a period of illness, families often choose music that reflects perseverance, peace and trust in God's promise. Gentle and familiar hymns can help express both gratitude for a life lived and hope in eternal rest.

Commonly Chosen Hymns

- **On Eagle's Wings**
  - Frequently chosen for its imagery of protection and rest.
- **Be Not Afraid**
  - Reflects reassurance and steady trust in God's presence.
- **Amazing Grace**
  - A familiar hymn of hope and redemption.
- **I Am the Bread of Life**
  - Often sung during Communion, centred on eternal life.
- **The King of Love My Shepherd Is**
  - Based on Psalm 23, reflecting guidance and lasting care.

Reflective Music (Where Permitted)

After a long illness, some families choose a gentle reflective piece before or after the Mass to acknowledge the journey that has been walked.

Always confirm with your parish what is appropriate within the liturgy.

Personal Tribute Songs (Outside the Mass)

Some families wish to include a contemporary song that reflects personality, friendship or personal memories. While these songs may hold deep meaning, they are usually more appropriate before or after the Mass, at the graveside, or during a memorial gathering.

Examples sometimes chosen include:

- **Choir**
- Often selected when themes of friendship and remembrance are central.
- **See You Again**
- Sometimes chosen when the focus is on reunion and enduring connection.
- **You Raise Me Up**
- Frequently used as a reflective tribute outside the formal liturgy.

Parish approval should always be confirmed before including non-liturgical music within a church service.

Putting It All Together: A Simple Planning Checklist

When time is limited, it can help to see the entire structure of the service in one place. The checklist below may be used when meeting with your priest or minister.

You do not need to choose everything alone. This guide is designed to help you feel prepared and confident.

Catholic Funeral Mass Structure

☐ First Reading (Old Testament)
 ☐ Responsorial Psalm
 ☐ Second Reading (New Testament)
 ☐ Gospel (usually chosen by the priest, but preferences may be discussed)
 ☐ Prayers of the Faithful

Music Selections

☐ Entrance Hymn
 ☐ Responsorial Psalm (if sung)
 ☐ Offertory Hymn
 ☐ Communion Hymn
 ☐ Recessional Hymn
 ☐ Reflective or Personal Tribute Song (if permitted)

Additional Considerations

☐ Who will proclaim the First and Second Readings?

   ☐ Who will read the Prayers of the Faithful?

   ☐ Is a eulogy or words of remembrance permitted?

   ☐ Are there parish guidelines regarding music?

   ☐ Are there any cultural or family traditions to consider?

Bring this checklist with you to your meeting. It can help ensure that every element feels personal and intentional.

Meeting with the Priest or Minister – What to Expect

Meeting with your priest or minister can feel overwhelming, especially if decisions need to be made quickly. Remember that their role is to guide you through the process with care and experience.

In most Catholic parishes, the meeting will include:

- Confirming the structure of the service
- Selecting the readings
- Discussing music choices
- Clarifying who will read or participate
- Reviewing any parish-specific guidelines

You may also be asked about:

- The life and faith of the person who has died
- Particular devotions or traditions
- Whether a eulogy or words of remembrance will be included

It is perfectly acceptable to bring notes or this guide with you. Having selections in mind can help the conversation feel calmer and more focused.

If you feel unsure about a choice, ask for guidance. Priests and ministers are accustomed to helping families in difficult moments.

Above all, remember that the purpose of the service is to honour the life of the person who has died and to proclaim Christian hope.

A Final Reflection

When my own family faced the loss of someone we loved, we had very little time to make decisions. We wanted every reading, every prayer and every hymn to feel meaningful — not chosen simply because it was familiar, but because it reflected a life that mattered deeply to us.

In the midst of grief, making these decisions felt heavier than expected. There were many options available, yet little clarity about where to begin.

This guide was written to offer calm structure in moments when clarity is difficult to find.

You do not need to choose the most complex reading. You do not need to select something dramatic or unfamiliar. The most meaningful choice is often the one that feels steady, personal and true to the life being honoured.

If this guide has helped you approach these decisions with even a little more confidence or peace, then it has served its purpose.

May the service you prepare reflect both the dignity of the life remembered and the hope that sustains us.

About the Author

Veronica Ruff writes practical, faith-informed guides designed to support individuals and families during significant life moments.

Drawing on personal experience and a background in healthcare, she understands how overwhelming important decisions can feel when time is limited. Her work focuses on clarity, structure and calm guidance, particularly within Catholic and Christian contexts.

Through Integrity Press, she develops resources that are thoughtful, accessible and pastorally sensitive.

Other Titles by Veronica Ruff

Veronica Ruff has also written additional faith-informed resources designed to offer guidance and reassurance during significant life moments.

These include practical guides for reflection, devotion and personal growth within Catholic and Christian contexts.

For further information about available titles, readers may visit Integrity Press or their preferred bookseller.

A Note to Readers

If this guide has been helpful to you during a difficult time, you may wish to leave a brief review with your bookseller. Your feedback can help other families find calm guidance when they need it most.

www.ingramcontent.com/pod-product-compliance
Lightning Source LLC
Chambersburg PA
CBHW031359060726
47590CB00007B/2858